PANDA

Written by
Jill Bailey

Illustrated by
Alan Baker

GALLERY BOOKS

An Imprint of W. H. Smith Publishers Inc.
112 Madison Avenue
New York City 10016

This series is concerned with the world's endangered animals, the reasons why their numbers are diminishing, and the efforts being made to save them from extinction. The author has described these events through the eyes of fictional characters. Although the situations described are based on fact, the people and the events described are fictitious.

A Templar Book

First trade edition published in the USA in 1990 by GALLERY BOOKS, an imprint of W.H. Smith Publishers Inc., 112 Madison Avenue, New York, New York 10016.

First trade edition published in Canada in 1990 by W.H. Smith Ltd, 113 Merton Street, Toronto, Canada M45 1A8.

Gallery Books are available for bulk purchase for sales promotions and premium use. For details write or telephone the Manager of Special Sales, W.H. Smith Publishers, Inc., 112 Madison Avenue, New York, New York 10016. (212) 532-6600.

Devised and produced by The Templar Company plc, Pippbrook Mill, London Road, Dorking, Surrey RH4 1JE, Great Britain.

Color separations by Positive Colour Ltd, Maldon, Essex, Great Britain. Printed and bound in Italy by OFSA S.p.a., Milan, Italy

ISBN 0-8317-7826-1

82-404   (1991-92)

CONTENTS

A PANDA IN THE KITCHEN
page 6

WINTER IN THE MOUNTAINS
page 18

TRACKING THE PANDA
page 30

PANDA UPDATE
page 44

INDEX
page 46

A PANDA
IN THE KITCHEN

Qin Zisheng stood at her kitchen door. Across the valley the wind was chasing the mist up the mountains, swirling between the tall spruce and fir trees. At least the rain had stopped. By the end of the month the weather would change, and the skies over these mountains in northwest Sichuan would clear.

Qin Zisheng had almost used up the pile of logs set aside for the cooking fire. She turned to her elderly mother, who was sitting by the fire.

"I'll go and collect some more logs after lunch," she said. "Will you look after Xiao Ling for me?" The old lady nodded. Little Xiao Ling ran across to her mother.

"Perhaps you'll see a panda," she said, hopefully. "Li Junji says they are coming very close to the village these days."

That summer, everyone in the village had marveled when the green stems of the bamboo suddenly burst into flower, their silky tassels swinging in the breeze. Bamboos flower only every 40 to 100 years. After they have set seed, they turn brown and die.

The bamboo is the panda's main food, and now that it had died away the pandas were starving. They were coming out of hiding in their desperate search for food. It would be several years before the new bamboo seedlings were big enough to provide food for such large animals as pandas.

Giant Pandas live high up in the mountains of the Sichuan, Gansu, and Shaanxi provinces in China.

Bamboo is the giant panda's staple diet. It flowers only rarely.

"Grandma's seen a panda, haven't you, Grandma?" she asked.

"When I was younger," said the old lady, "pandas were quite a common sight on our farm. Some people thought pandas could drive away evil spirits. They put pictures of pandas outside their houses at night to protect them."

"Why aren't there so many pandas now?" asked Xiao Ling.

"They like to stay in the forest and feed on bamboos," said her grandmother. "In those days there were not so many farms, and there were many patches of bamboos between the farms. Now the whole hillside is covered in fields."

"Didn't the bamboo die, too?" asked Xiao Ling.

"Yes," replied her grandmother, "but not all kinds of bamboos die at the same time. In the old days, different kinds of bamboos grew further down the mountains. When one kind died, the pandas moved down into the valleys and ate the others. They can't do that now because of the farms."

There are 700 kinds of bamboo but the panda prefers only two, the arrow and the umbrella bamboo. This panda is in the typical eating position – sitting.

"That's why our cousins have had to leave their farm, isn't it?" asked Xiao Ling. "So that they can plant new bamboo forests to help the pandas."

Xiao Ling's cousins lived in a large village. All the people had been moved to a new village further down the valley. The Chinese government had paid for the move. At first, the people were not happy about moving, but the new houses had electricity for cooking and

Pandas once lived in many parts of China, but vast areas of forest have been cut down for wood and to grow crops. These vegetable plots are in the Sichuan province.

heating. They would no longer need to collect wood from the forest and so disturb the pandas. Now the foresters from the Panda Reserve were planting new forests on the old fields. These forests would take a long time to grow.

After the family had eaten their midday soup, Qin Zisheng set out to collect the firewood. Soon she was in the dim, quiet world of the forest. The tall, dark firs and spruces seemed to reach up into the mist.

Long stems of bamboo towered above her, dripping with moisture from the recent rain. Qin Zisheng peered at every clump of bamboo,

The panda's forest habitat is cold, damp and dense. Between the thickets of bamboo are tall fir, spruce, and birch trees. Lichens and mosses grow on every surface.

hoping to get a glimpse of a panda. She looked in vain. The bamboos were so dense that she would not have seen a panda unless she'd fallen over it.

Suddenly, she noticed some tracks in the wet mud – panda footprints. Not far away there was a large pile of dung, like a heap of dark turnips, full of spiky pieces of undigested bamboo. Qin Zisheng began to follow the tracks.

The trail led toward a large, hollow spruce tree. She paused. This was the time of year when female pandas gave birth to their babies. Qin Zisheng did not want to come face to face with an angry mother panda nearly 5 feet tall and weighing 220 pounds. She could hear moaning and grunting sounds coming from the den. The panda was at home.

Qin Zisheng waited and waited, hoping the panda would come out of its den. But it didn't. It began to rain again; it was getting cold and mist was curling down between the trees. Qin Zisheng decided to set off for home.

Mother pandas use large, hollow trees in which to give birth to their young. They can be very fierce if disturbed.

Six weeks had passed since Qin Zisheng had found the panda's den and the first snows of winter lay on the mountains. There had been more reports of starving pandas. A group of loggers who had been felling trees further up the mountain told them how the pandas used to visit the campsite in the evenings, to steal food. They were so hungry that they would eat almost anything. The loggers had taken pity on them and left out scraps of meat. Pandas like meat, but they are too slow and clumsy to catch most animals.

One morning, while Xiao Ling was waiting for her breakfast, she heard a strange noise outside. She crept to the window – and there it was, a panda, sitting in the yard beside an upturned trashcan! Like a large, cuddly bear, the panda sat comfortably on its haunches, nibbling at some vegetable peelings. It looked thin. Its fur was matted, and seemed to hang in folds from its body, but to Xiao Ling it was her own special panda. She rushed off to tell her mother.

Qin Zisheng knew just what to do. She poured some warm porridge into a large iron pot and took it out to the panda.

The panda lapped up three bowls of porridge, then it leaned back against the wall of the kitchen, folded its paws across its tummy, and went to sleep. It slept for a very long time.

Qin Zisheng gave the panda warm porridge to eat. Pandas are usually very shy animals, but now they were being driven to the village by their hunger.

In winter, snow covers the mountain slopes of the panda's home. The temperature is well below freezing, but the panda is protected from the cold by its thick fur.

While the panda slept, watched over by little Xiao Ling, Qin Zisheng sent for the panda rescue squad. Since the great bamboo die-back of 1974, when hundreds of pandas had died, every village in the panda reserves had its own specially-trained panda rescue team. Soon they came puffing up the hill, carrying a large cage made of wooden poles. They dragged the sleeping panda into the cage. The cage was then so heavy that it took five men to lift it.

The panda woke up with a jolt, but it was so weak that it was unable to put up much of a fight. It was cross that its slumbers had been disturbed and made a strange huffing sound. Xiao Ling was very upset to see "her" panda being taken away.

"Why can't we keep it?" she asked her mother.

"It will need a lot of food – lots of bamboo and porridge, perhaps for many months," said Qin Zisheng. "At the Panda Research Center they will know how to look after it properly. When it is well again, they will let it go in a part of the forest where it will be able to find enough food."

Xiao Ling was still upset when her father, Qin Hua, came home from work later that day.

"Cheer up," he said. "I have a

Recent education programs have taught people who live in the reserves that they should look after pandas. People who help starving pandas are rewarded.

surprise for you. Tomorrow we are going to visit the Panda Research Center. Then you will be able to see your panda again, and all the other pandas that have been rescued from the forest."

The panda rescue team dragged the sleeping panda into the cage, then carried it back to the Research Center. An adult panda can weigh up to 330 lbs.

The Research Center was home to several pandas that had been rescued from starvation. It was set high on a hillside overlooking a wild valley. Xiao Ling's panda had been nicknamed Porridge, because that was what he liked to eat. Porridge's large cage opened onto a patch of hillside surrounded by an escape-proof fence. There were several clumps of trees for the pandas to climb. Porridge was sitting in a corner munching his way through a very large pile of bamboo shoots.

"See how he uses his paws to tear back the leaves and break open the stems," said his keeper, and he pushed a new piece of bamboo into the cage. Porridge grabbed at it greedily. Gripping it firmly with one paw, the panda neatly stripped off the leaves, bent the thick stem in half, and snapped it open. Then he tore at it with his large sharp teeth, to get at the soft pith in the middle of the stem.

"How much bamboo does he eat?" asked Xiao Ling.

The panda doesn't have a real thumb, like humans do, but it has a kind of sixth finger, formed from one of its wrist bones. It uses this to grip things.

"Four to five hundred stems a day," replied the keeper, "about 44 pounds. The trouble is, pandas do not digest plant food very well. To get the nutrients they need from bamboo, they have to eat huge amounts of it. That's why they produce so many large droppings."

Xiao Ling understood why she had not been allowed to keep the panda. Imagine having to go out into the forest and collect 500 stems of bamboo every day. No wonder pandas need a lot of forest to live in!

Pandas rescued from starvation are either moved to areas where the bamboo is not flowering, or, like those above, kept in captivity. It is a costly operation.

WINTER IN THE MOUNTAINS

Chu Ching, the director of the Panda Research Center, stepped out of his office and looked across the valley. His visitor, the French zoologist, Maurice Gaillard, followed him. The clouds were lifting, and the snow sparkled in the sunshine.

"This will be a good day to show you around the Reserve," said Chu Ching. He held out a large map of the area. "This is one of the largest panda reserves. It stretches far up into the mountains toward Tibet. Unfortunately, it is not all good

Chu Ching and Maurice Gaillard studied the map of the Reserve. The map represented 770 square miles of panda habitat.

habitat for pandas. There are no trees on the mountain tops."

"Where does the bamboo grow?" asked Maurice.

"It grows throughout the forest," replied Chu Ching, "wherever the sunlight can get through the trees. There are several different kinds of bamboos growing at different levels up the hillsides. The pandas, however, seem to prefer to feed on the kind that grows higher up the mountains."

"Is this the biggest panda reserve?" asked Maurice. He could see range upon range of mountains in the distance.

"Yes," said Chu Ching. "There are 11 others scattered across Sichuan province and the southern part of Gansu province. Pandas

have lived here ever since the Ice Age, over 30,000 years ago."

"So they prefer ice and snow?" asked Maurice.

"No," replied Chu Ching. "Once there were many more pandas in China. They could be found as far as Beijing. The climate was wetter, and bamboos grew in many places

The Panda Research Center at Wolong in the Sichuan province. The Center breeds captive pandas and has its own veterinary hospital.

that are now covered in fields. Even here, pandas used to come down into the valleys before the farmers built their terraces there."

Chu Ching and Maurice Gaillard started to walk up the mountain. They could hear the sound of rushing water in the valley below.

"Pandas always live near water," said Chu Ching. "They need to drink every day. In this weather the mountain streams may be frozen over, so the pandas will have to come down to the valleys."

"Do you often watch pandas in the wild?" asked Maurice.

"No," replied Chu Ching. "They are very difficult to see, especially in the snow. Even the great zoologist George Schaller, who

Dr George Schaller with Chinese workers at a research station in the Wolong Nature Reserve. In 1980, Dr Schaller helped to set up a panda research project which is still at work.

came here to study the pandas, did not see one for two months. He was out in the hills every day looking for them." He pointed to some tracks in the snow. "In the snow, however, it is easy to find their tracks."

Beside the track was a large lump of dung. Chu Ching scooped it up and put it into a plastic bag.

"We will take this home with us," he said. "It will tell us what kind of bamboo the panda has been eating. The size of the bamboo pieces in it will tell us the panda's age. If the panda has worms or other parasites they too will appear in the dung. We may even find the bones of bamboo rats – sometimes the pandas are quick enough to catch them."

They followed the panda's tracks down to the stream, where the panda had paused to drink.

Pandas always live near water. They need to drink every day. In winter, when the mountain streams freeze, pandas come down to the valleys to drink.

Back at the Research Center, Lee Ta Ming, the chief forester, had also noticed the fine weather. He decided to go into the forest to collect soil samples. He crossed the stream and climbed high up the mountain. From time to time he stopped to scoop up some soil into a bag.

Suddenly Lee Ta Ming heard a rustle in the undergrowth. He spun around, fearing it might be a leopard. There was a loud clap of wings and a brilliantly colored pheasant flew up from under his feet. Lee Ta Ming leapt out of the way, tripped over a root and fell heavily to the ground. He felt a flash of pain in the lower part of his leg – he had twisted his ankle. It was already beginning to swell. How could he get back to the center? If he stayed out on the mountain all night in this weather, he would probably freeze to death. He began to feel very frightened.

Down by the river, Maurice Gaillard suddenly looked up.

"Listen! The river sounds different," he remarked.

A golden pheasant flew out from under Lee Ta Ming's feet. He leapt out of the way, tripped over a root and fell heavily to the ground.

Chu Ching paused to listen. Then he glanced at the mountain across the valley.

"No – it's not the river," he said. "Someone is calling and the sound is echoing in the valley. We must go and see if he needs help."

The snub-nosed monkey is one of the many animals that shares the forest with the panda. In order to save the giant panda, its natural home must be preserved and with it the great variety of plants and animals that live there.

Lee Ta Ming sat very quietly as the panda began to feed. It reared up on its hind legs and pulled the tall bamboo over until it snapped.

Lee Ta Ming sat down at the foot of a large spruce tree. Exhausted by shouting and by the pain in his ankle, he fell asleep.

Suddenly, he awoke. Something was moving near him; he could hear the bamboos rustling. To his amazement there was a large panda only a short distance away, feeding on the bamboo.

As Lee Ta Ming watched, the panda slowly rose to its feet, reared up on its hind legs, and reached for the top of a tall bamboo, pulling it over until it snapped.

There was a distant shout, and the panda dropped to the ground. Silently, it slid away through the undergrowth. Lee Ta Ming sat up and shouted as hard as he could at the distant voices. He sighed with relief when, in a short while,

he saw Maurice and Chu Ching emerging from the thick bamboo.

A little while later, the three men made their way slowly down the mountain. Lee Ta Ming hopped on one leg, supported by his friends. They were disappointed to have missed the panda. After a while, Lee Ta Ming wanted to rest, as his ankle was hurting a lot.

"You never know," he said, "if we sit quietly, we may be lucky enough to see another panda."

He lay back against a tree trunk

A panda eats bamboo by pushing the stem into the corner of its mouth and taking several quick bites while jerking the stem up and down to break it.

and watched the clouds drifting over the tree tops. Then he saw a small figure silhouetted against the sky. An animal was climbing high up in a fir tree, its long tail dangling below the branches.

"I've found you another panda," he whispered to the others.

Maurice and Chu Ching looked up sharply, saw only the empty forest around them, and scowled at Lee Ta Ming.

"That's not a very funny joke," said Chu Ching, sourly.

"It's not a joke," said Lee Ta Ming, "but it's not a giant panda. It's a red panda. Look up there."

Some scientists believe that the red panda is the giant panda's closest relative. It lives in the same areas as the giant panda, but eats leaves, fruit, acorns, and eggs.

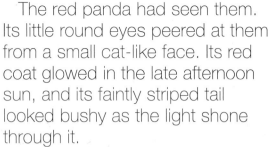

The red panda had seen them. Its little round eyes peered at them from a small cat-like face. Its red coat glowed in the late afternoon sun, and its faintly striped tail looked bushy as the light shone through it.

"The panda's closest relation," remarked Chu Ching.

"Surely the red panda is related to the raccoons," protested Maurice. "I've always thought the giant panda was a bear."

"You could be right," replied Chu Ching. "The panda's Chinese name, *da xiongmao*, means 'big bear cat.' Nobody is really quite sure whether the panda is a bear or a raccoon. Some people have decided to put it in a family of its own."

"It looks like a bear that is camouflaged for living where there is snow," said Maurice.

"Yes," agreed Chu Ching, "but this part of the world has snow for only three months of the year, so its camouflage is no use most of the time. Anyway, the panda doesn't really have any enemies, except humans. It is usually only sick or very old pandas that are attacked by other animals."

Right: pandas are excellent climbers. Their sharp claws enable them to cling to trunks and branches.

Lee Ta Ming disagreed.

"Some people think the panda's bold black and white pattern has the opposite effect," he said. "It helps the pandas to notice each other in the thick bamboo."

"Why would they want to do that?" asked Maurice.

"Pandas don't like company," said Lee Ta Ming. "If the pandas lived too close together, there wouldn't be enough bamboo to go around. So they try to avoid each other. Also, they do not digest their food very well. Even if a panda feeds for 13 or 14 hours a day, it only just gets enough to eat, so it must save energy. If it can avoid meeting other pandas, it will not waste energy in arguments or fights."

Maurice had been carrying Lee Ta Ming's heavy bag.

"What have you got in here?" he asked.

"Soil specimens," replied Lee Ta Ming. "At the Research Center we are trying to find out whether other kinds of bamboos can grow here. At the moment, there are only two kinds of bamboo in the Reserve. If we can plant some different kinds, they won't all flower at the same time, and the pandas won't starve when the shoots die back."

Left: a researcher examines the broken stems left behind by a feeding panda. Information about how pandas feed is an important part of the struggle to save them.

In the past, pandas could move to another species of bamboo if one kind dies back. Now, fields and houses separate one patch of forest from another.

TRACKING THE PANDA

Spring had arrived. The birches were putting out tender green leaves, and the rhododendrons were flowering, producing splashes of red, pink, and purple on the hillside. Soon the pandas would be looking for mates.

Hu Mingjiang, a young zoologist studying panda behavior, had promised to show Maurice how to track pandas. The previous autumn, Hu Mingjiang had captured five pandas and put radio collars on them. The collars sent out signals which could be picked up by a radio antenna. In this way, the researchers could find out exactly where the pandas were. The two men would spend a month in the depths of the forest.

"Pandas do not usually travel very far," said Hu Mingjiang. "They keep to a home area of about 4 square miles.

They looked for a suitable place to pitch their tent.

"We need to be on a ridge," said Hu Mingjiang. "Then the hills will not get in the way of the radio signals. This is a good area. There are plenty of panda signs here."

"I don't see any," said Maurice, peering at the ground for footprints.

"Over there, on that tree trunk," said Hu Mingjiang. "Do you see the dark marks at the bottom of the trunk? Also, the bark has been rubbed smooth. It is a scent post."

This was obviously a good place for studying pandas, so the two men built a firm platform of logs, and pitched their tent on it. Then they went to have a closer look at the panda's scent post.

Pandas due to be fitted with a radio collar are first caught in a log trap. This is baited with rotting meat.

In the winter, the bamboo forests are
cold and damp. Researchers have
to build camps in which they can
live comfortably for many months.

Maurice remarked that he could smell a faint odor.

"Yes, that's the panda's smell," said Hu Mingjiang. "Pandas produce a smelly liquid just under their tails. They rub this on tree trunks and the smell tells other pandas they are near. Their large furry tails help to spread the scent around, something like a paint brush. Look," he pointed to some deep cuts in the bark just above the black patch, "the pandas often scratch the bark as they leave their scent. These marks are fresh – you can see the chips of bark on the ground below."

"Is it only male pandas that make a scent mark?" asked Maurice.

"Most of the time, yes," replied Hu Mingjiang. "Females scent mark at this time of year, that is, when they are looking for a mate."

The sun was setting, and it was getting very cold as Maurice and Hu Mingjiang finished their supper.

"Shall we test the antenna and see if there are any pandas around?" suggested Hu Mingjiang.

He stood outside the tent holding the radio antenna, while Maurice adjusted the signal-receiving set. Hu Mingjiang turned the antenna in different directions. Suddenly, Maurice picked up a signal – "Beep, beep, beep!"

"That's Shao-Shao, a young female panda," said Hu Mingjiang.

The panda is caught, put to sleep and fitted with a radio collar. It does not hurt, and the animal soon gets used to wearing the collar.

"The beeps are quite fast. That means she is moving around, probably feeding."

"Do pandas always feed at night?" asked Maurice.

"They feed at any time of day," replied Hu Mingjiang, "but they are at their most active around dawn and sunset."

From research stations in the heart of the reserve, researchers study how pandas live. Here, a scientist looks into a mother panda's den.

Pandas mark their territory by leaving scent on tree trunks. This panda is checking whether it has entered another panda's territory.

The following afternoon, they picked up Shao-Shao's signals again. Then, as Hu Mingjiang turned the antenna in another direction he picked up a different signal.

"This should be Chang-Chang, a large male," he said. "The signals show that he is close to Shao-Shao's home area. Perhaps he is looking for a mate."

After two hours, Hu Mingjiang had picked up signals from four of his five pandas. There was no sign of the fifth. This was a mystery. As they were discussing whether to search for him, strange sounds echoed across the valley, the deep

The radio transmitter in the panda's collar is powered by a tiny battery, but its signals can be picked up by an antenna some distance away.

sounds of a panda trying to attract a mate.

"Let's go and look for it," said Hu Mingjiang.

With the radio receiver strapped on to Hu Mingjiang's back and the antenna in his hand, the two men set off down the hillside in the direction of the pandas. As the signals on the receiver became stronger, they moved more slowly, and very quietly. They could now hear two pandas calling. They were very close. Hu Mingjiang signaled to Maurice to stop, and pointed between two large fir trees. There was one of the pandas. Around her neck, they saw the yellow radio collar. She was pacing up and down restlessly.

"That's Shao-Shao," whispered Hu Mingjiang. "She is five and a half years old, just old enough to become a mother."

The calls of the male panda grew louder and louder, and then Chang-Chang lumbered into sight.

Researchers weighing a panda before fitting a radio collar. Studying pandas in the wild is not easy. They are shy animals and hard to find in dense forest.

As Chang-Chang approached, Shao-Shao barked at him as if she were a dog. Chang-Chang backed away, then slowly moved toward her again. This time, Shao-Shao lunged out at him, her paws narrowly missing his face.

"I thought she wanted to see him," whispered Maurice.

"She does," replied Hu Mingjiang, "but pandas are so used to avoiding each other that it will take her a little time to get used to his being so close."

After Chang-Chang had made several approaches, Shao-Shao became less worried, and began to moan, a gentle moan that rose and fell. Then, the two men again heard low calls in the distance. Another panda was approaching.

"When female pandas call for a mate, the sound attracts males from all around," whispered Hu Mingjiang.

Another, smaller male panda came into sight.

"That's Zhen-Zhen," said Hu Mingjiang, "the panda whose signal was missing. See – he has lost his radio collar."

Chang-Chang roared at his rival, and made as if to attack him. Zhen-Zhen retreated, then crept forward again. The two pandas faced each other for some time,

while Shao-Shao looked on. She was not at all interested in the newcomer. Zhen-Zhen eventually wandered off, disappointed.

Chang-Chang and Shao-Shao moved off together into some dense bamboos, out of sight. The two men could hear them making gentle bleating sounds.

"They are going to mate, I think," said Hu Mingjiang.

Only during the mating season do male and female pandas meet each other. They often begin courtship by fighting and then follow with a series of calls including grunts, growls, snarls, and pants.

"Female pandas are very particular about their mates," whispered Hu Mingjiang. "Even if there is only one male around, they will not mate with him if they don't like him. It's one of the reasons why they breed so slowly. Shao-Shao will be ready to mate on only three days every year. If she does not find a mate she likes in that time, she will not look again for another year. Even if she does mate, she may not necessarily get pregnant."

"If Shao-Shao gets pregnant," said Maurice, "when will the baby panda be born?"

"Not for another 14 to 23 weeks," replied Hu Mingjiang. "Then it will need constant attention. Very young pandas are often killed by leopards or hyaenas while their mothers are away feeding."

As they drew closer to the camp, Maurice suddenly tripped and fell, with a howl of pain. His foot was trapped in a wire noose. Hu Mingjiang rushed to free him.

"Poachers!" he exclaimed angrily. "They are after musk deer. Scent from their musk glands fetches very high prices – it is used in Chinese medicines." He took out his handkerchief to mop up the blood that was now oozing from Maurice's foot. "Pandas get caught in these traps, too. They die because they starve or because the wound gets infected."

The next day they returned to the Research Center to attend to Maurice's wound.

Maurice had caught his foot in a snare. Had he been a struggling animal the wire would soon have cut into his ankle.

The snare that caught Maurice had been set for musk deer. These animals are endangered and yet they are still killed for their musk glands. Like Maurice, pandas are often caught in these snares.

Back at the Research Center, Hu Mingjiang showed Maurice the captive pandas and the operating theater where they saved sick pandas or helped the females who were having trouble producing young. There were also laboratories for the scientists and a veterinary hospital.

"Who provides the money for all this?" asked Maurice.

"The Chinese government," replied Hu Mingjiang, "and the World Wide Fund for Nature (WWF), and other conservation groups from all over the world.

"Nobody realized the pandas were in danger until 1949, when a Hong Kong newspaper ran a story about them, pointing out that their natural home was being destroyed for farming at an alarming rate. The Chinese government immediately banned all hunting of pandas. Between 1963 and 1983, 12 special panda reserves were created. In 1974, a large number of pandas died when the bamboo flowered, and the news spread around the world. Then in 1979, Sir Peter Scott from the WWF came to set up the 'Save the Panda' campaign."

Several months later, two months before Maurice was due to return to France, one of the female pandas at the Center started pacing up and down her cage. She pushed pieces of bamboo around as if trying to make a nest. She was pregnant. Her keepers watched her carefully, using a remote-controlled camera so as not to disturb her. As the birth approached she began to moan.

Newborn pandas are pink and hairless. They are about 6 in long and weigh 3 1/2-5 oz. In a month they have the familiar black and white markings.

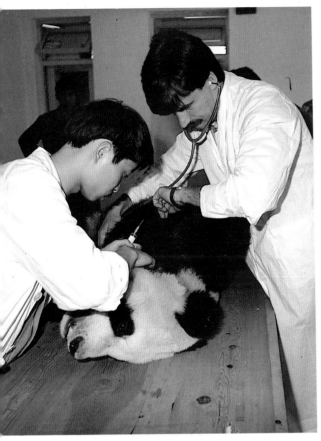

Eventually, the moaning stopped. There was a high-pitched squeal, and then another. The squeals were those of her two tiny offspring.

"A mother panda usually produces twins," said Hu Mingjiang, "but she can only look after one; the other will die."

Veterinarians, left, treating a panda in the Wolong Research Center. Pandas breed so slowly in the wild that a great effort is made to breed them successfully in captivity.

Sir Peter Scott with a panda in the Wolong Nature Reserve. Sir Peter was a founder member of the WWF and set up the "Save the Panda" campaign in 1979.

As Hu Mingjiang had predicted, only one of the panda's young survived. It was so tiny that it was lost in its mother's fur as she cuddled it close to her breast to give it some milk.

"Its eyes will be closed," said Hu Mingjiang. "They won't open for another month. It has very little fur, just pink skin."

After a month, the baby panda had grown a black and white coat. Only now did his mother let go of him, and then only for a short time. Until now she had cuddled him even when she was feeding.

"He won't stand until he is at least ten weeks old," said Hu Mingjiang.

"Are many pandas born in captivity?" asked Maurice.

"Only a few," said Hu Mingjiang, "and they often die within a few weeks. Most zoos have only one or two male pandas, and the females are so choosy about their mates. There are about 100 pandas in zoos all over the world. Some people think they should be returned to the wild because there are so few pandas left and because they do not breed successfully in zoos. But they attract visitors, and that attracts money to help them. Also, scientists can study pandas in zoos, and learn more about how they live and behave. This will help us to protect them in the wild. China does not allow many pandas to leave the country now."

Hu Mingjiang and Maurice thought of Shao-Shao up in the forest and wondered if she, too, was cuddling a new baby panda.

Pandas are very popular in zoos. The visitors' money goes toward saving the panda. Unfortunately, pandas have not bred very successfully in zoos outside China.

To the Chinese, the panda is a national treasure. To the rest of the world, it is also a symbol. It stands for the need to conserve the natural world which is our home too.

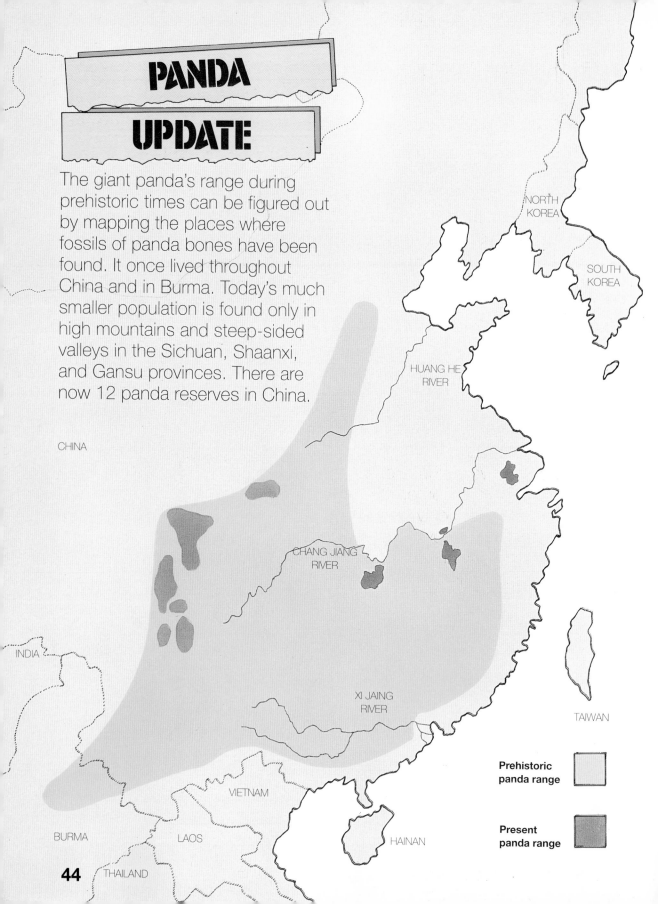

PANDA
UPDATE

The giant panda's range during prehistoric times can be figured out by mapping the places where fossils of panda bones have been found. It once lived throughout China and in Burma. Today's much smaller population is found only in high mountains and steep-sided valleys in the Sichuan, Shaanxi, and Gansu provinces. There are now 12 panda reserves in China.

CHINA

NORTH KOREA

SOUTH KOREA

HUANG HE RIVER

CHANG JIANG RIVER

INDIA

XI JAING RIVER

TAIWAN

VIETNAM

BURMA

LAOS

HAINAN

THAILAND

Prehistoric panda range

Present panda range

THE PROBLEM PANDA

The giant panda seems almost doomed to extinction. Almost every feature of its biology is against it. The reasons are as follows:

● The panda feeds on only one or two species of bamboo. In the past, pandas could move to other parts of the forest when the bamboo in their immediate area died. Due to loss of habitat, pandas now live in isolated patches of forest; they cannot migrate and so they starve.

● The panda's body is not well-suited to its vegetarian diet. It has to eat large amounts of bamboo to get enough nourishment.

● Pandas breed very slowly, only rearing one young at a time.

● Female pandas are only able to mate for about 3 days every year and are very choosy about mates.

● Many pandas die in snares set for musk deer. They are also poached for their skins. In the remote mountains where they live it is difficult to protect them from poachers.

Who are the panda's closest relatives?

For over a century people have argued over the giant panda's relatives. When a panda is seen walking slowly up a hill, it looks very much like a bear, yet when you look at its face while it is feeding, it looks quite cat-like, with its blunt nose and round flattened cheeks. The common Chinese name for the panda, *da xiongmao* means "big bear-cat", so even the Chinese are confused.

The giant panda shares its homeland with the much smaller red panda, which also feeds on bamboo as well as fruit, nuts, and roots. The red panda lives in trees, and is closely related to the raccoons of the Americas.

Raccoon

Red panda

Chemical studies of the panda and of living and fossil bears have now shown that the panda is most closely related to the bears.

Spectacled bear

INDEX

B

babies 11, 38, 40-1, 42
bamboo 6, 8-10, 14, 16-19, 24, 28-9, 40, 45
bamboo rats 21
bears 26, 45
Beijing 19
birches 10, 30
birth 11, 40-1
breeding 38, 41, 42, 45
Burma 44

C

climbing 26, 27
conservation groups 40
courtship 37
crops 8-9

D

den 12, 33
drinking 21
dung 11, 17, 21

E

education programs 14
extinction 45

F

farms 8, 9, 19
feeding 6, 8, 12, 24-5, 28-9, 33, 45
firewood 9, 10
firs 10, 25
fur 12, 13, 42

G

Gansu province 6, 18, 44
government 9, 40

H

habitat 10, 18, 45

L

lichens 10
loggers 12
log trap 30

M

mating 30, 32, 34-8, 45
mosses 10
musk deer 38-9, 45

P

panda rescue squad 14-15
Panda Research Center 14-16, 18-19, 22, 28 38, 40
panda reserves 9, 14, 18, 28
parasites 21
pheasant 22
poachers 38, 45

R

racoon 26, 45
radio collars 30, 34-6
red panda 26, 45
research stations 33
researchers 30-9
rhododendrons 30

S

"Save the Panda" campaign 40-1
scent post 30, 32-3
Schaller, Dr. George 20-1

Scott, Sir Peter 40-1
Shaanxi province 6, 9, 18, 19, 44
size 11, 15, 40
smell 32-3
snares 38-9, 45
snow 12-13, 26
snub-nosed monkey 23
soil samples 22, 28
spruce 10, 11

T

territory 33
Tibet 18
tracking 30-4
tracks 11, 21

V

veterinary hospital 19, 40-1
village 6, 9, 14

W

water 20
Wolong Nature Reserve 19, 20, 41
World Wide Fund for Nature 40, 41

Z

zoos 42